Really Easy Guitar!

Bob Dylan

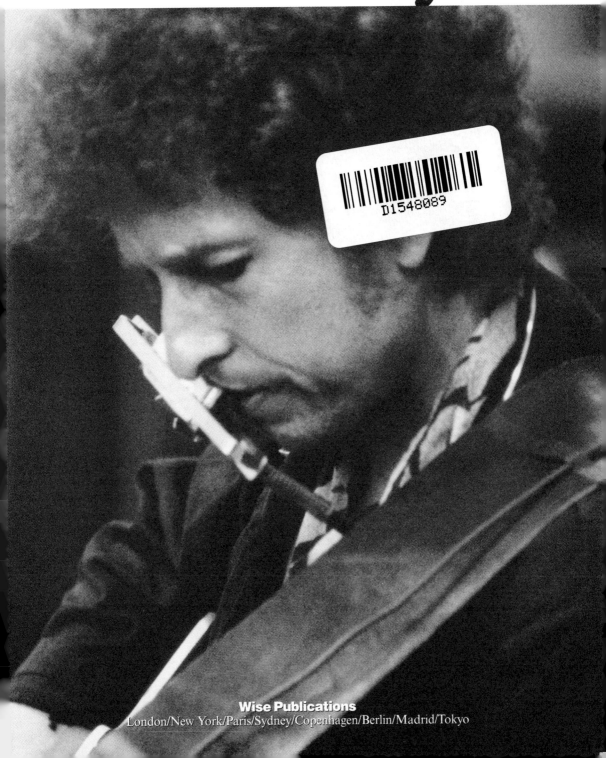

Wise Publications
London/New York/Paris/Sydney/Copenhagen/Berlin/Madrid/Tokyo

Contents

Exclusive distributors:
Music Sales Limited
8/9 Frith Street, London W1D 3JB, England.
Music Sales Corporation
257 Park Avenue South
New York NY10010 USA
Music Sales Pty Limited
120 Rothschild Avenue, Rosebery,
NSW 2018, Australia.

Order no. AM971828
ISBN: 0-7119-9062-X
This book © 2002 by Wise Publications

Written and arranged by Joe Bennett
Additional research by Paul Morris
and Jill Warren
Music Processed by The Pitts and Paul Ewers
Edited by Sorcha Armstrong
Book design by Chloë Alexander
Cover and book photographs courtesy of
Redferns/Ken Regan
Pages 3-6 photographs by George Taylor

Printed in the United Kingdom by
Printwise (Haverhill) Limited, Haverhill, Suffolk.

CD mastered by Jonas Persson
Guitars by Arthur Dick

Your Guarantee of Quality
As publishers, we strive to produce every book to the highest commercial standards.
The music has been freshly engraved and the book has been carefully designed to minimise awkward page turns and to make playing from it a real pleasure. Particular care has been given to specifying acid-free, neutral-sized paper made from pulps which have not been elemental chlorine bleached. This pulp is from farmed sustainable forests and was produced with special regard for the environment.
Throughout, the printing and binding have been planned to ensure a sturdy, attractive publication which should give years of enjoyment. If your copy fails to meet our high standards, please inform us and we will gladly replace it.

Got any comments?
e-mail reallyeasyguitar@musicsales.co.uk

Introduction

Welcome to Really Easy Guitar, a fantastic new way to learn the songs you love.

This book will teach you how to play 11 great Bob Dylan songs – and you don't even have to be able to read music!

Inside you will find lyrics and chords for each song, complete with the chord shapes you need to start playing immediately. There's a special introduction to each song, with helpful hints and playing tips. Fretboxes and guitar TAB teach you the famous riffs and patterns that everyone will recognise.

The accompanying 12-track CD features professionally recorded soundalike versions of each song – vocals have been left off so that you can sing along.

Just follow the simple four step guide to using this book and you will be ready to play along with your favourite musician!

1 Tune Your Guitar

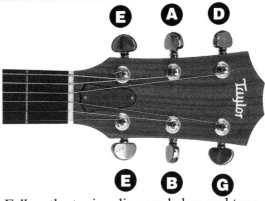

Before you can start to play along with the backing tracks, you'll need to make sure that your guitar is in tune with the CD. Track 1 on the CD gives you notes to tune to for each string, starting with the top E string, and then working downwards.

Alternatively, tune the bottom string first and then tune all the other strings to it.

Follow the tuning diagram below and tune from the bottom string upwards.

6th to 5th string	5th to 4th string	4th to 3rd string	3rd to 2nd string	2nd to 1st string

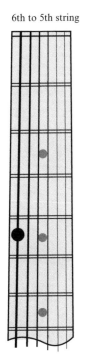

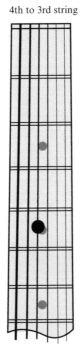

2 Understanding fretbox diagrams

Throughout this book, fretbox diagrams are used to show chord shapes and scale patterns. Think of the box as a view of the fretboard from head on – the thickest (lowest) string is on the left and the thinnest (highest) string is on the right.

The horizontal lines correspond to the frets on your guitar; the circles indicate where you should place your fingers.

An x above the box indicates that that string should not be played; an o indicates that the string should be played open.

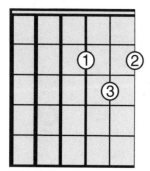

So, when you're playing this chord of D, make sure that you don't hit the bottom two strings.

All the chords you need for each song are given at the top of the song, in the order that they appear in that song.

Shapes that are played higher up the neck are described in the same way – the lowest fret used is indicated to the left of the box. A curved line above the box shows that a first finger barre should be used.

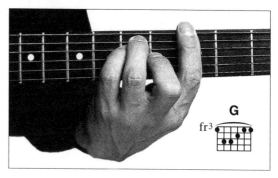

This barre chord of G is played at the third fret, with the first finger stretching across all six strings.

3 Understanding scale patterns

We can also use chord box diagrams to show you certain useful scale patterns on the fretboard. When a box is used to describe a scale pattern, suggested fingerings are also included.

Black circles show you the root note of the scale. If the root note of the scale is an open string, this is indicated by a double circle. Grey circles represent notes of the scale below the lowest root note.

So in this example, the root note of the scale is the open D string, with another D appearing at the third fret on the B string.

4 Understanding TAB

TAB is another easy way to learn the famous riffs and hooks in each song. The six horizontal lines represent the six strings of the guitar – the lowest line represents the lowest string (low E), while the highest line represents the highest string (high E). The number on each line tells you which fret should be played.

Although we've also included traditional music notation, you don't actually need to be able to read music to use TAB – just listen to the recording and follow the fret positions on the TAB and you'll soon be playing along. There are certain special symbols which are used:

Hammer-on

Look out for a slur connecting two numbers – when the second number is higher than the first this is called a "hammer-on". Place one finger at the lower of the two frets indicated and pick that string, then, without picking the string again, place your next finger at the higher fret. You should hear a smooth change in sound between the two notes.

Pull-off

A Pull-off is the opposite of a hammer-on, and is denoted by a slur joining two TAB numbers, where the second number is lower than the first one.

Place your fingers at the two fret positions indicated, and pick the first (higher) note, then simply lift the top finger, without picking the string again, allowing the bottom note to ring out.

Slide

A slide between two notes is denoted by a short line in the TAB. Simply play the first note, and then move your finger to the new fret position by sliding it along the fretboard, restriking the string as you arrive at the new position.

Legato slide

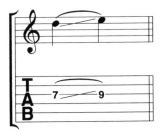

A legato slide is exactly the same as a normal slide, except that the second note is not picked again.

Bend

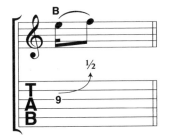

String bends are indicated as shown above – the amount that you need to bend the string is indicated near the arrow and could be ¼ tone (a decorative bend), ½ tone (the equivalent of one fret) or 1 tone (the equivalent of two frets).

Palm Muting

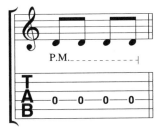

To get this percussive effect, place the side of your picking hand against the strings near the bridge as you pick.

2 Like A Rolling Stone

from *Highway '61 Revisited* (1965)

BETWEEN 1962 AND EARLY 1965 Bob Dylan was regarded by many of his fans as a folk singer. Then he released the all-electric album *Highway '61 Revisited* and everything changed - he was even booed off stage for appearing live with an electric guitar. When you hear the subtle clean picking parts of 'Like A Rolling Stone' it's hard to understand what the fuss was all about, although Bob typically didn't try to build bridges with his lost fans – at the time he was quoted as saying "Folk music is just a bunch of fat people".

Guitar parts

The song features two guitarists – Bob himself playing chords, with Mike Bloomfield playing the electric lead licks. The two guitar parts play in different positions on the neck, one covering mainly open chord shapes, the other playing fretted barre shapes and adding lead guitar fills. An acoustic strums in the background throughout.

How to play it

Before you start, note that Bob has a particular way of playing the open C chord (see TAB). Practise this shape until it's as comfortable to play as a regular C. Then, rather than strumming all the strings up and down, pick one note at a time from the chord, with an 8-to-the-bar rhythm. Take a listen to the CD to hear how this rhythm sounds. We've notated the first four bars of the verse to get you started.

Guitar sound

The electric guitar sound is very bright so that it can cut through the thick mix of guitars, bass, drums and Hammond organ, so select the bridge pickup on your guitar. Turn the guitar's tone and volume up full, and turn the mid and treble controls on your amp just past 12 o'clock. Back off the bass control slightly, and finally add reverb (use the amp's own reverb if you've got it; if you're using pedal effects, set your reverb to a 'Hall' setting, and turn it up to around 30% of the clean sound level). Most important, though, is the picking technique. Use a plectrum, and ensure that you fret each chord cleanly without a hint of fret buzz – this way, you'll stand a better chance of achieving that 'chiming' arpeggio sound on the original.

▼ Verse accompaniment style

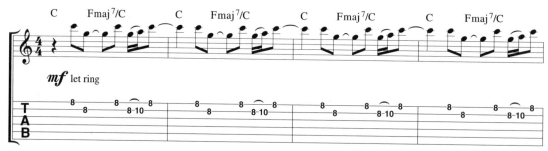

"I find C major to be the
key of strength, but also the key of regret.
E major is the key of confidence.
A♭ major is the key of renunciation."

2 Like A Rolling Stone

Words & Music by Bob Dylan

C   Fmaj⁷   Dm   Em   G   F

Intro
| C   Fmaj⁷ | C   Fmaj⁷ | C   Fmaj⁷ | C   Fmaj⁷ ‖

Verse 1

    C   Dm
Once upon a time you dressed so fine,

       Em   F   G
You threw the bums a dime in your prime,   didn't you?

    C   Dm   Em
People'd call, say "Beware, doll, you're bound to fall,"

                F   G
You thought they were all   a-kidding you.

F   G
   You used to   laugh about

F   G
   Everybody that was   hanging out.

F   Em   Dm   C
   Now you don't talk so loud,

F   Em   Dm   C
   Now you don't seem so proud,

   Dm   F   G
About having to be scrounging   your next meal.

Chorus 1

           C   F   G
How does it feel,

           C   F   G
How does it feel,

             C   F   G
To be without a home

                C   F   G
Like a complete unknown,

            C   F   G
Like a rolling stone?

Link
| C   F | G | G   ‖

Verse 2

         C   Dm   Em
You've   gone to the finest school alright, Miss Lonely,

       F   G
But you know you only used to get juiced in it.

      C   Dm   Em
Nobody's ever taught you how to live out on the street

           F   G
And now you're gonna have to get used to it.

F   G
   You said you'd never compromise

F   G
   With the mystery tramp but now you realise

F   Em   Dm   C
   He's not selling any alibis ___

F   Em   Dm   C
As you stare into the vacuum of his eyes

    Dm   F   G
And say "Do you want to make a deal?"

Chorus 2

              C   F G
How does it feel,

              C   F G
How does it feel,

                C   F G
To be on your own

                 C   F G
With no direction home,

              C   F G
A complete unknown,

              C   F G
Like a rolling stone?

Link

| C   F | G | G   ‖

Verse 3

         C   Dm
You   never turned around to see the frowns

Em   F
   On the jugglers and the clowns

                 G
When they all did tricks for you.

      C   Dm
You never understood that it ain't no good,

      Em   F   G
You shouldn't let other people get your kicks for you.

cont.

F
You used to ride on the chrome horse with your   diplomat   **G**

F   **G**
Who carried on his shoulder a   Siamese cat.

F   **Em**   **Dm**   **C**
Ain't it hard   when you discover that

F   **Em** **Dm**   **C**
He really wasn't where it's at

Dm
After he took from you everything

F   **G**
He could steal? ___

Chorus 3

           C   **F** **G**
How does it feel,

           C   **F** **G**
How does it feel,

            C   **F** **G**
To be on your own

               C   **F** **G**
With no direction home,

             C   **F** **G**
Like a complete unknown,

          C   **F** **G**
Like a rolling stone?

Link | **C** **F** | **G** | **G** ||

Verse 4

C   **Dm**   **Em**
Princess on the steeple and all the   pretty people

             F   **G**
They're all drinking, thinking that they   got it made,

C   **Dm**
Exchanging all   precious gifts

Em   **F**
But you'd better take your diamond ring,

G
You'd better pawn it babe.

F   **G**
You used to be   so amused

F   **G**
At Napoleon in rags   and the language that he used.

    F   **Em**   **Dm**   **C**

Go to him now, he calls you, you can't refuse,

    F   **Em**   **Dm**   **C**

When you got nothing you got   nothing to lose.

    Dm

You're invisible now, you got no secrets

    F   **G**

To conceal. _____

Chorus 4

                  C   **F** **G**

How does it feel,

                  C   **F** **G**

How does it feel,

                  C   **F** **G**

To be on your own

                    C   **F** **G**

With no direction home,

                   C   **F** **G**

Like a complete unknown,

                C   **F** **G**

Like a rolling stone?

Coda   ‖: **C**   **F** | **G** | **C**   **F** | **G**   :‖   *Repeat to fade*

3 Tombstone Blues

from *Highway '61 Revisited* (1965)

FOR THE FIRST SEVEN tracks on *Highway '61 Revisited* Bob used blues virtuoso Mike Bloomfield to add those controversial electric lead guitar parts. Only on 'Tombstone Blues' do you hear Mike truly getting an opportunity to play blues lead guitar throughout.

▼ F♯m pentatonic scale

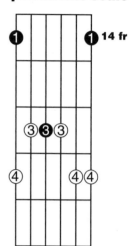

How to play it

Despite the title, the song's chords don't bear much resemblance to a traditional 12-bar blues format. There are only two chords in the song – F♯ and B (although their equivalents F♯7 and B7 are used at times to add variation). The chorus doesn't feature a 'turnaround' (i.e. a chord pattern taking you back to the start) – instead, the band simply jam around the F♯ chord until Bob's ready to sing the next verse.

Acoustic guitars

Bob's using a rapid strumming pattern that repeats every bar – D D DU D – with slight variations. Listen carefully to the intro and you'll hear that there are actually two acoustic guitars – one in the left speaker and one in the right. The left side plays the strumming pattern, and the right focuses on single downstroke strums in time with the snare drum. You can choose to play either part – the chord shapes are identical. Note that in the chord sheet the F♯s become Es and the Bs become As – simply put a capo on the 2nd fret to play the acoustic part.

Lead lines

It's unusual for a Bob Dylan song to feature so much lead guitar, so let's take a look at how Mike Bloomfield played those classy blues licks. The fretbox shows a scale shape of F♯ minor pentatonic. Mike uses all of the notes from this scale to improvise phrases. Try bending the third (G) string up at the 16th fret for added blues authenticity. The same scale shape can also be used 12 frets lower down the neck (at the 2nd fret) – Mike starts verse 1 in this position, then moves to the higher position at the end of the first chorus.

Guitar sound

The electric guitar sound is typical electric blues – bridge pickup into slightly distorted guitar amp, and reverb added. Make sure the guitar's volume and tone are up full so that you drive the amp hard enough to achieve that biting blues tone. If the audience don't like it – well, they're probably just 'fat folkies'…

▼ Intro lead licks

"I haven't changed a bit.
I just got tired of playing the guitar by myself."

3 Tombstone Blues

Words & Music by Bob Dylan

E7	A7	A	E

Capo 2nd fret

Intro ‖: E7 | E7 | E7 | E7 :‖

Verse 1

E7   A   E
The sweet pretty things are in bed now of course

                    A   E
The city fathers they're trying to endorse

                 A   E
The reincarnation of Paul Revere's horse

              A   E
But the town has no need to be nervous.

                 A   E
The ghost of Belle Starr she hands down her wits

             A   E7
To Jezebel the nun she violently knits

                A   E
A Bald wig for Jack the Ripper who sits

            A   E
At the head of the chamber of commerce.

Chorus 1

A7   E7
Mama's in the fac'try she ain't got no shoes
A7   E7
Daddy's in the alley he's lookin' for the fuse
A7   E7
I'm in the street with the tombstone blues.

Verse 2

            G   A   E
The hysterical bride in the penny arcade
                    A   E
Screaming she moans, "I've just been made"
      E   A   E
Then sends out for the doctor who pulls down the shade
                A   E
Says, "My advice is not to let the boys in."
                        A   E
Now the medicine man comes and he shuffles inside
                    A   E
He walks with a swagger and he says to the bride
                A   E
"Stop all this weeping, swallow your pride
            A   E
You will not die it's not poison."

Chorus 2

A7   E7
Mama's in the fac'try she ain't got no shoes
A7   E7
Daddy's in the alley he's lookin' for the fuse
A7   E
I'm in the kitchen with the tombstone blues.

Verse 3

<pre>
                              A   E
Well, John the Baptist after torturing a thief
                        A   E
Looks up at his hero the Commander-in-Chief
                        A   E
Saying, "Tell me great hero, but please make it brief
                        A   E
Is there a hole for me to get sick in?"
     E   A   E
The Commander-in-Chief answers him with a chasing fly
                        A   E
Saying, "Death to all those who would whimper and cry"
                     A   E
And dropping a bar bell he points to the sky
                     A   E
Saying, "The sun's not yellow it's chicken."
</pre>

Chorus 3   *As Chorus 1*

Verse 4

<pre>
     E   A   E
The king of the Philistines his soldiers to save
                           A   E
Put jawbones on their tombstones and flatters their graves
                        A   E
Puts the pied pipers in prison and fattens the slaves
                   A   E
Then sends them out to the jungle.
     E   A   E
Gypsy Davey with a blowtorch he burns out their camps
                        A   E
With his faithful slave Pedro behind him he tramps
             A   E
With a fantastic collection of stamps
                   A   E
To win friends and influence his uncle.
</pre>

Chorus 4   *As Chorus 1*

Verse 5

                  A   **E**
The geometry of innocent flesh on the bone
        A   **E**
Causes Galileo's math book to get thrown
                A   **E**
At Delilah who's sitting worthlessly alone
              A   **E**
But the tears on her cheeks are from laughter.
                      A   **E**
Now I wish I could give Brother Bill his great thrill
                    A   **E**
I would set him in chains at the top of the hill
                    A   **E**
The send out for some pillars and Cecil B. DeMille
            A   **E**
He could die happily ever after.

Chorus 5   *As Chorus 1*

Guitar solo   *(Improvise over E7)*

Verse 6

                                 A   **E**
Where Ma Raney and Beethoven once unwrapped their bed roll
                     A   **E**
Tuba players now rehearse around the flagpole
                              A   **E**
And the National Bank at a profit sells road mapss of the soul
                  A   **E**
To the old folks home and the college
                      A   **E**
Now I wish I could write you a melody so plain
                        A   **E**
That could hold you dear lady from going insane
                            A   **E**
That could ease you and cool you and cease the pain
                    A   **E**
Of you useless and pointless knowledge.

Chorus 6   *As Chorus 1*

4 I Want You

from *Blonde On Blonde* (1966)

ONLY EIGHT MONTHS after Bob released the all-electric *Highway '61 Revisited* he was back, this time with one of rock's earliest double albums. He later described the album as "…my sound. I haven't been able to succeed in getting it all the time". Staying firmly with the electric feel, 'I Want You' uses no fewer than five guitarists, including Robbie Robertson (the *Blonde On Blonde* backing lineup eventually became The Band) and Joe South (who was later to compose Deep Purple's 'Hush' among other classics).

How to play it

The 5th fret capo'd guitar picking of the intro continues almost throughout the entire song, so we've shown the first eight bars to get you started. It was originally played fingerstyle (with thumb picking the bass notes). If you find this too difficult try picking the notes with the plectrum and leaving out any tricky bass notes – these will be covered by at least one of the remaining four guitar parts!

Guitar sound

Use a bright, clean sound, ideally using a guitar with single-coil pickups (e.g. Fender Stratocaster). Turn the volume and tone controls on the guitar up full, back off the bass control on the amp, and add reverb to the end result. If you own a compressor you may want to use a subtle setting to help the notes ring out more clearly.

▼ **Main guitar part**

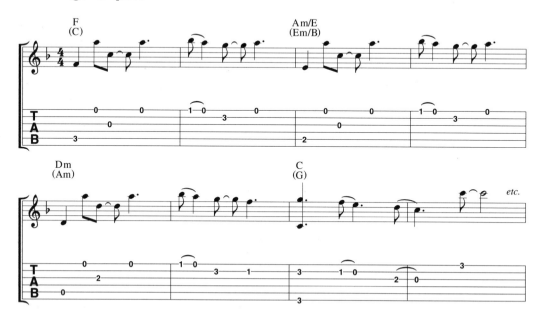

I Want You

Words & Music by Bob Dylan

C   Em/B   Am   G   Em/B   F

Capo 5th fret

Intro

| C | C | Em/B | Em/B |

| Am | Am | G | G |

| C | C | C | C |

Verse 1

    C
The guilty undertaker sighs,
    Em/B
The lonesome organ grinder cries,
    Am   G
The silver saxophones say I should refuse you.
    F
The cracked bells and washed-out horns
G
   Blow into my face with scorn,
    Am
But it's not that way,
          G
I wasn't born to lose you.

Chorus 1

   C   Em/B
I want you, I want you,
  Am   G
I want you so bad,
        C
Honey, I want you.

Verse 2

      C
The drunken politician leaps

    Em/B
Upon the street where mothers weep

      Am
And the saviours who are fast asleep,

  G
They wait for you.

    F
And I wait for them to interrupt

   G
Me drinkin' from my broken cup

   Am
And ask me to

     G
Open up the gate for you.

Chorus 2   *As Chorus 1*

     Em
Bridge   Now all my fathers, they've gone down

Am
True love they've been without it.

   Em
But all their daughters put me down

    F   **G**
'Cause I don't think about it.

    C
Verse 3   Well, I return to the Queen of Spades

Em/B
And talk with my chambermaid.

Am
She knows that I'm not afraid

  G
To look at her.

F
   She is good to me

    G
And there's nothing she doesn't see.

   Am
She knows where I'd like to be

     G
But it doesn't matter.

| *Chorus 3* | *As Chorus 1* |

Verse 4

             C
Now your dancing child with his Chinese suit,

   Em/B
He spoke to me, I took his flute.

Am
No, I wasn't very cute to him,

G
  Was I?

   F
But I did it, though, because he lied

G
  Because he took you for a ride

Am
  And because time was on his side

   G
And because I…

| *Chorus 4* | *As Chorus 1* |

Outro

| **C** | **C** | **Em/B** | **Em/B** |

| **Am** | **Am** | **G** | **G** | *Repeat to fade*

5 Just Like A Woman

from *Blonde On Blonde* (1966)

IT IS SAID THAT 'Just Like A Woman' was written about 1960s model and art-film star Edie Sedgwick. As well as starring in many of Andy Warhol's films (and appearing at his equally legendary parties) she was linked to Lou Reed, Mick Jagger and Dylan himself before her drug-related death in 1971. The song's lyrics describe her chaotic lifestyle in the song as "like all the rest, with her fog, her amphetamine and her pearls". It's possible that two other Dylan songs – 'Like a Rolling Stone' and 'Leopardskin Pillbox Hat' were also about Edie.

How to play it
There are six guitarists credited on the original recording including Dylan himself, but the track is mainly driven by a single arpeggio-based classical guitar part (see TAB). This is quite difficult to play accurately, especially if you're new to fingerstyle guitar, so as with all challenging guitar parts, the best plan is to start slowly and gradually build up to speed.

The thumb covers the bass notes of each chord, and the three fingers pick one string each. After a little practice this technique is actually easier than picking the notes one at a time with the plectrum. Note that the difficult barre chords shown in the TAB are actually easier to play on a classical guitar because of the lower string tension. Once you can play the intro as shown, try devising a picking part for the rest of the song using barre chord shapes around the 5th-9th fret area.

Easy version
Many players will find the classical part too challenging – indeed, it was well beyond Bob's own mid-60s guitar playing ability – so here's an alternative method of playing the song. Play the open chord shapes shown in the fretboxes over the page, strumming four slow downstrokes per bar, and let the CD backing track take the trickier arpeggio parts. Once you've mastered this, try throwing in occasional upstrokes to make the rhythm more interesting – listen to the snare drum part on the CD track for inspiration.

▼ Opening bars

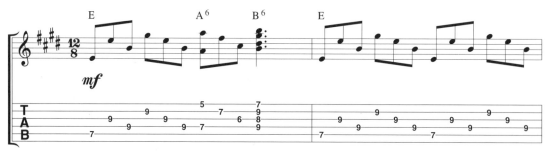

Just Like A Woman

Words & Music by Bob Dylan

Intro
| E   A B7 | E | E   A B7 | E ||

Verse 1

    E   A   B7 E   Esus4 E
Nobody feels any pain

          A   B7   E   Esus4 E
Tonight as I stand inside the rain,

A   B7   A   B7
Everybody knows that baby's got new clothes

     A G♯m F♯m E   B7
But late - ly   I   see her ribbons and her bows

       C♯m E   A B7
Have fallen from her curls.

Chorus 1

      E   G♯m F♯m E   A
She takes just like   a   woman, yes she does,

      E   G♯m F♯m E   A
She makes love just   like   a   woman, yes she does,

        E   G♯m F♯m E   A
And she aches just   like   a   woman,

        B7   E
But she breaks just like a little girl.

Link
| A* E* A* B | E* ||

Just Like A Woman

Verse 2

<pre>
          E   A   B7 E   Esus4 E
Queen Mary, she's my friend.
                  A   B7 E   Esus4 E
Yes, I believe I'll go see her again.
      A   B7   A   B7
Nobody has to guess that baby can't be blessed
      A G#m F#m E   B7
Till she finally sees that she's like all the rest
            C#m   E   A   B7
With her fog, her amphetamine   and her pearls.
</pre>

Chorus 2

<pre>
       E   G#m F#m E A
She takes just like   a   woman, yes,
       E   G#m F#m E   A
She makes love just like   a   woman, yes she does,
           E   G#m F#m E A
And she aches just like   a   woman,
           B7   E
But she breaks just like a little girl.
</pre>

Link

<pre>
| A* E* A* B | E* ||
</pre>

Bridge

<pre>
       G#7
It was raining from the first

And I was dying there of thirst
       E
So I   came in here.
           G#7
And your   longtime curse hurts
                           A
But what's worse is this pain in here,
B7
   I can't stay in here,

Ain't it clear:
</pre>

Verse 3

      E A B7 E   Esus4 E
That I just can't fit.

                      A   B7   E   Esus4 E
Yes, I believe it's time for us to quit.

A   B7   A   B7
When we meet again, introduced as friends,

A   G♯m F♯m E B7
Please don't let on that you knew me when

        C♯m   G♯m A B7
I was hungry and it was your   world.

Chorus 3

        E   G♯m F♯m E A
Ah you fake just like a woman, yes you do,

        E   G♯m F♯m E A
You make love just like a woman, yes you do,

            E G♯m F♯m E A
Then you ache just like a woman,

        B7   E
But you break just like a little girl.

Link | **A* E* A* B** | **E*** ||

Coda | **E   A B7** | **E   Esus4 E** | **E   A B7** | **E   Esus4 E** |

          | **A   B7** | **A   B7** | **A G♯m F♯m E** | **B7** |

          | **C♯m E A** | **B7** | **E G♯m F♯m E** | **A** |

          | **E G♯m F♯m E** | **A** | **E G♯m F♯m E** | **A** |

          | **B7** | **A* E* A* B** | **E*** ||

6 Stuck Inside Of Mobile With The Memphis Blues Again

from *Blonde On Blonde* (1966)

IN TYPICALLY esoteric fashion, Dylan described the *Blonde On Blonde* album as having "that thin, that wild mercury sound. It's metallic and bright gold, with whatever that conjures up…". 'Memphis Blues Again' is certainly a great example of his sound at the time, with its strong folk-rock strummed acoustic part and constant electric guitar riff.

How to play it

Bob's own acoustic guitar part is the easiest option, consisting of a repeating strumming pattern – DUDU UDU – throughout each bar. Keep your strumming hand moving across the strings in a relaxed motion, and hold the plectrum loosely so that the strings don't restrict each strum. If you find this difficult (or keep dropping the plectrum!), try using a thinner one and holding it more firmly. Pivot from the elbow rather than the wrist, and strum with confidence. Don't worry if you occasionally deviate from the exact strumming pattern – Bob does too!

Electric guitar part

If you know your barre chords, you'll see that the main riff (see TAB) is based on a 7th fret barre chord of E. Guitarist Wayne Moss picks the three 9th fret notes that form the E 'partial chord', then uses a rapid hammer-on and pull-off riff with the little finger at the 12th fret while holding down the 9th fret notes. You'll need a light touch here, and it may take a good deal of practice before you can play this riff exactly in time with the track (listen to our soundalike CD version to get the exact timing).

Guitar sound

Dylan is playing an acoustic guitar with heavy strings and a fairly high action, which is what gives the *Blonde On Blonde* original its brash intro tone. Generally you should always buy acoustic strings that are as heavy as your fingers can stand, as this always makes for a better tone.

The electric guitar sound is less bright than other songs on the album. Select the middle or neck pickup position, and back off the tone slightly on the guitar. Use a minimal amount of reverb (so you can *just* hear it when you're playing along to the track) and pick the riff delicately to avoid fret buzz and out-of-tune strings.

▼ Electric guitar riff

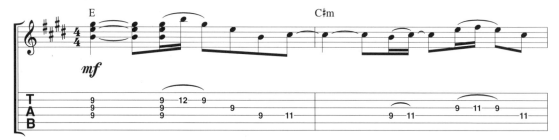

"If has that thin, that wild mercury sound.
It's metallic and bright gold, with whatever
that conjures up…"

6 Stuck Inside Of Mobile With The Memphis Blues Again

Words & Music by Bob Dylan

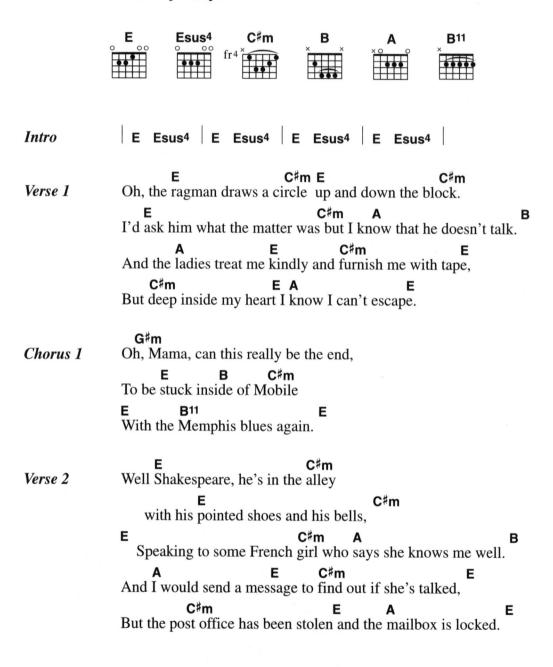

E   Esus4   C#m   B   A   B11

Intro

| E Esus4 | E Esus4 | E Esus4 | E Esus4 |

Verse 1

           E   **C#m E**   **C#m**
Oh, the ragman draws a circle up and down the block.

     E   **C#m**   **A**   **B**
I'd ask him what the matter was but I know that he doesn't talk.

         A   **E**   **C#m**   **E**
And the ladies treat me kindly and furnish me with tape,

   C#m   **E A**   **E**
But deep inside my heart I know I can't escape.

Chorus 1

   G#m
Oh, Mama, can this really be the end,

      E   **B**   **C#m**
To be stuck inside of Mobile

E   **B11**   **E**
With the Memphis blues again.

Verse 2

      E   **C#m**
Well Shakespeare, he's in the alley

        E   **C#m**
with his pointed shoes and his bells,

E   **C#m**   **A**   **B**
Speaking to some French girl who says she knows me well.

     A   **E**   **C#m**   **E**
And I would send a message to find out if she's talked,

     C#m   **E**   **A**   **E**
But the post office has been stolen and the mailbox is locked.

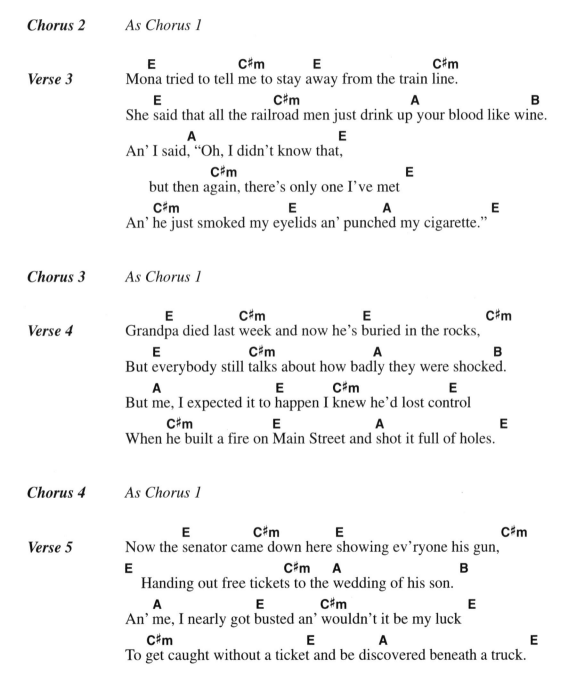

Chorus 2   *As Chorus 1*

                     E   C#m   E   C#m
Verse 3   Mona tried to tell me to stay away from the train line.
                     E   C#m   A   B
                She said that all the railroad men just drink up your blood like wine.
                            A   E
                An' I said, "Oh, I didn't know that,
                               C#m   E
                    but then again, there's only one I've met
                      C#m   E   A   E
                An' he just smoked my eyelids an' punched my cigarette."

Chorus 3   *As Chorus 1*

                            E   C#m   E   C#m
Verse 4   Grandpa died last week and now he's buried in the rocks,
                     E   C#m   A   B
                But everybody still talks about how badly they were shocked.
                      A   E   C#m   E
                But me, I expected it to happen I knew he'd lost control
                            C#m   E   A   E
                When he built a fire on Main Street and shot it full of holes.

Chorus 4   *As Chorus 1*

                            E   C#m   E   C#m
Verse 5   Now the senator came down here showing ev'ryone his gun,
                E   C#m   A   B
                    Handing out free tickets to the wedding of his son.
                            A   E   C#m   E
                An' me, I nearly got busted an' wouldn't it be my luck
                      C#m   E   A   E
                To get caught without a ticket and be discovered beneath a truck.

Stuck Inside Of Mobile With The Memphis Blues Again

Chorus 5   *As Chorus 1*

Verse 6

          E   C♯m
Now the team preacher looked so baffled
         E   C♯m
  when I asked him why he dressed
E   C♯m   A   B
With twenty pounds of headlines stapled to his chest.
      A   E
But he cursed me when I proved to him,
    C♯m   E
  then I whispered, "Not even you can hide.
   C♯m   E A   E
You see, you're just like me, I hope you're satisfied."

Chorus 6   *As Chorus 1*

Verse 7

          E   C♯m
Now the rainman gave me two cures,
      E   C♯m
  then he said, "Jump right in."
  E   C♯m   A   B
The one was Texas medicine, the other was just railroad gin.
    A   E   C♯m   E
An' like a fool I mixed them an' it strangled up my mind,
       C♯m   E   A   E
An' now people just get uglier an' I have no sense of time.

Chorus 7   *As Chorus 1*

Verse 8

          E   C#m   E   C#m
When Ruthie says come see her in her honky-tonk lagoon,

          E   C#m   A   B
Where I can watch her waltz for free 'neath her Panamanian moon.

        A   E
An' I say, "Aw come on now,

            C#m   E
  you know you know about my debutante."

            C#m   E
An' she says, "Your debutante just knows what you need

        A   E
  but I know what you want."

Chorus 8   *As Chorus 1*

Verse 9

              E   C#m   E   C#m
Now the bricks lay on Grand Street where the neon madmen climb.

      E   C#m A   B
They all fall there so perfectly,   it all seems so well timed.

      A   E   C#m   E
An' here I sit so patiently waiting to find out what price

C#m   E   A   E
You have to pay to get out of going through all these things twice.

Chorus 9   *As Chorus 1*

Outro | E | E | E | Esus⁴ |

           | E   B | C#m E | B¹¹ B | E |

33

7 Visions Of Johanna

from *Blonde On Blonde* (1966)

BOB DYLAN'S LYRICS have been pored over and written about by self-appointed 'Dylanologists' for almost forty years. 'Visions of Johanna' is a typical example of the kind of writing that got the rock critics in late-60s America so excited. At over seven minutes, it's the second longest track on *Blonde On Blonde*, and the band's sparse accompaniment is understated through all five verses to allow Dylan's poetic imagery to come to the fore.

How to play it

First of all, if you're going to play along to the backing track you'll need a capo at the 2nd fret – the song is in the key of A, but all the acoustic guitar chord shapes are based around chords of G, C and D. Next, get your strumming hand used to the rhythmic acoustic riff. It's a simple idea that uses one bar strummed in a '16s' rhythm, and the second bar strumming in '8s'. This pattern is shown in full in the TAB below.

Bob's chords

As well as having a trademark 'C' chord (see 'Like A Rolling Stone') Bob also often plays a chord of G using a shape you rarely find in chord books (see fretbox). You'll almost certainly find this shape uncomfortable to fret at first, but persevere – it's essential if you're going to use your first finger at the first fret in bar 1 of the riff.

Electric guitar part

The two electric guitars on the recording take different roles. The first plays a rhythmic 'skank' (off-beat) using barre chords of A, D and E, using a very bright sound with very little reverb. The second guitar throws in occasional lead lines, improvised from the A minor pentatonic scale (see fretbox 2). This is an equally bright (bridge pickup) sound, using compression and reverb. Tip – lots of the improvised licks begin with a bend on the third string, 7th fret. In some of the later verses, this becomes a double bend on the second and third string at the same time. If this doesn't hurt, that means you're not doing it properly!

▼ **Bob Dylan G chord**

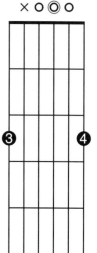

▼ **Am pentatonic scale shape**

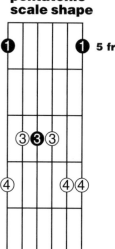

▼ **Acoustic guitar strumming pattern**

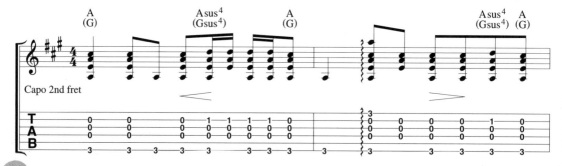

"I wear dark sunglasses.
There is no profound reason for it.
I like dark sunglasses."

7 Visions Of Johanna

Words & Music by Bob Dylan

G   C   D   Gsus4   Dsus4

Capo 2nd fret

Intro | G | G | Gsus4 D | G Gsus4 | G |

Verse 1

                                                     C

Ain't it just like the night to play tricks

                       D   G Gsus4 G

when you're tryin' to be so quiet?

                                   C   D   G Gsus4 G

We sit here stranded, though we're all doin' our best to deny it

              D   G Gsus4 G

And Louise holds a handful of rain, temptin' you to defy it

        C   G Gsus4 G

Lights flicker from the opposite loft

        C   G

In this room the heat pipes just cough

      C   G

The country music station plays soft

                                            D (Dsus4) D

But there's nothing, really nothing to turn off

                G   C   D   G   Gsus4 G

Just Louise and her lover so entwined

                 C   G   D   G Gsus4 G

And these visions of Johanna that conquer my mind.

Break | G | C D | G Gsus⁴ G | G |

Verse 2

                G   C   D
In the empty lot where the ladies play blindman's bluff
                  G
  with the key chain
                            C   D   G
And the all-night girls they whisper of escapades out on the "D" train
             D
We can hear the night watchman click his flashlight
                                   G   Gsus⁴ G
Ask himself it it's him or them that's insane
       C   G
Louise, she's all right, she's just near
       C   G
She's delicate and seems like the mirror
         C   G
But she just makes it all too concise and too clear
                 D Dsus⁴ D
That Johanna's not here
    G   C   D   G Gsus⁴ G
The ghost of 'lectricity howls in the bones of her face
                     C   G   D   G Gsus⁴ G
Where these visions of Johanna have now taken my place.

Break | G | C D | G Gsus⁴ G | G |

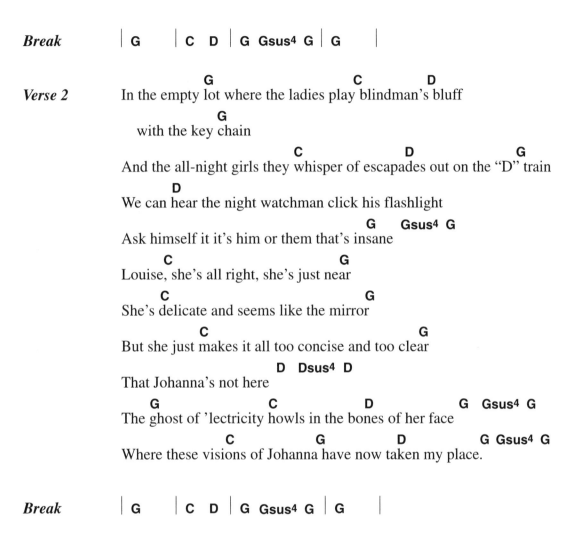

Verse 3

```
                                          C        D      G  Gsus4 G
(G)
Now, little boy lost, he takes himself so seriously
                        C        D         G   Gsus4 G
He brags of his misery, he likes to live dangerously
            D
And when bringing her name up
                          G   Gsus4 G
He speaks of a farewell kiss to me
        C            G  C              G
He's sure got a lotta gall to be so useless and all
        C                G              D   Dsus4 D
Muttering small talk at the wall while I'm in the hall
      G
How can I explain?
        C      D        G  Gsus4 G
Oh, it's so hard to get on
                  C      G            D           G  Gsus4 G
And these visions of Johanna, they kept me up past the dawn.
```

Break

```
| G    | C  D | G  Gsus4 G | G        |
```

Verse 4

```
                      C        D      G  Gsus4 G
Inside the museums, Infinity goes up on trial
                          C           D          G  Gsus4 G
Voices echo this is what salvation must be like after a while
            D
But Mona Lisa musta had the highway blues
                          G   Gsus4 G
You can tell by the way she smiles
        C                G
See the primitive wallflower freeze
          C               G
When the jelly-faced women all sneeze
          C               G
Hear the one with the mustache say, "Jeez
                   D  Dsus4 D
I can't find my knees"
      G            C             D           G
Oh, jewels and binoculars hang from the head of the mule
          C      G            D           G
But these visions of Johanna, they make it all seem so cruel.
```

Bridge | G | C D | G Gsus⁴ G | G |

Verse 5
                                                    C
               The peddler now speaks to the countess
                         D   G   Gsus⁴ G
                 who's pretending to care for him
                                                              C   D
               Sayin', "Name me someone that not a parasite and I'll go out and
                         G   Gsus⁴ G
                 say a prayer for him"
                         D
               But like Louise always says

               "You can't look at much, can ya man?"
                                        G
               As she, herself, prepares for him
                         C   G Gsus⁴ G
               And Madonna, she still has not showed
                         C   G Gsus⁴ G
               We see this empty cage now corrode
                         C   G   Gsus⁴ G
               Where her cape of the stage once had flowed
                         C   G Gsus⁴ G
               The fiddler, he now steps to the road
                         C   G   Gsus⁴ G
               He writes ev'rything's been returned which was owed
                         C   G Gsus⁴ G
               On the back of the fish truck that loads
                                        D   Dsus⁴ D
               While my conscience explodes
                         G   C   D   G Gsus⁴ G
               The harmonicas play the skeleton keys and the rain
                                   C   G   D   G Gsus⁴ G
               And these visions of Johanna are now all that remain.

8 Lay Lady Lay

from *Nashville Skyline* (1969)

IN 1969 DYLAN released the album *Nashville Skyline*, which was, as the name suggests, entirely recorded in that town, and consequently sounded unsurprisingly 'country'. He also moved away from the acerbic counter-culture lyrics of *Blonde On Blonde* to deliver a collection of simpler, more up-beat songs. 'Lay Lady Lay' is a straightforward love song with an unmistakeable Roy Orbison influence in both the lyric and its delivery.

▼ Double pull-off shape

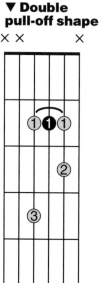

How to play it

The track is carried by a single picked acoustic guitar part, using the thumb and two fingers to pick rapid arpeggios (i.e. chords played one note at a time). The intro and verse accompaniment uses chords of A, C♯m, G and Bm. To create a very simple accompaniment you could strum each chord once on every beat – this sounds surprisingly effective over the backing track. If you want to play the same part as on the recording, take a look at the TAB below.

The thumb covers all of the notes on the fourth (D) string, and the first and second fingers play the third and second strings respectively. You should try to develop a 'rippling' motion so that the notes sound in groups of three. Start very slowly and gradually build up speed, ensuring that notes played by the thumb are the same volume as those covered by the fingers. The part is actually much more difficult than it sounds due to the rapid position changes combined with the speed of the picking.

Whatever colours...

The second section ("Whatever colours...") uses a similar picking pattern, but around chords of E and F♯m before returning to the A. At this point (just after "in your mind") all of the guitars play a double pull-off using a Rolling Stones-style chord shape (see fretbox). To play this you need to flatten the first finger over the second, third and fourth string at the 2nd fret, then add on the third and second fingers (shown in grey). Pluck the chord and pull off using both fingers at the same time, keeping your flattened finger on the second fret.

▼ Intro and verse picking part

"I don't know how important my work is.
It's not important to the average cat
who works eight hours a day.
What does he care?
The world can get along
very well without it.
I'm hip to that."

8 Lay Lady Lay

Words & Music by Bob Dylan

Chord diagrams: A (fr5), C#m (fr4), G (fr3), Bm (fr2), E, F#m, A*, D

Intro   ‖: A C#m │ G Bm :‖

Chorus 1
```
        A              C#m G        Bm              A   C#m G Bm
        Lay, lady, lay,    lay across my big brass bed.
        A              C#m G        Bm              A   C#m G Bm
        Lay, lady, lay,    lay across my big brass bed.
```

Verse 1
```
        E            F#m              A*
        Whatever colors you have in your mind,
        E                    F#m   A*
        I'll show them to you and you'll see them shine.
```

Chorus 2
```
        A            C#m G        Bm              A   C#m G Bm
        Lay, lady, lay,    lay across my big brass bed.
        A            C#m G              Bm        A C#m G Bm
        Stay, lady, stay,    stay with your man awhile.
        A                  C#m
        Until the break of day,
        G                Bm              A C#m G Bm
        Let me see you make him smile.
```

Verse 2
```
        E              F#m          A*
        His clothes are dirty but his hands are clean.
        E                F#m                A*
        And you're the best thing that he's ever seen.
```

Chorus 3
```
        A            C#m G          Bm          A C#m G Bm
        Stay, lady, stay,    stay with your man awhile.
```

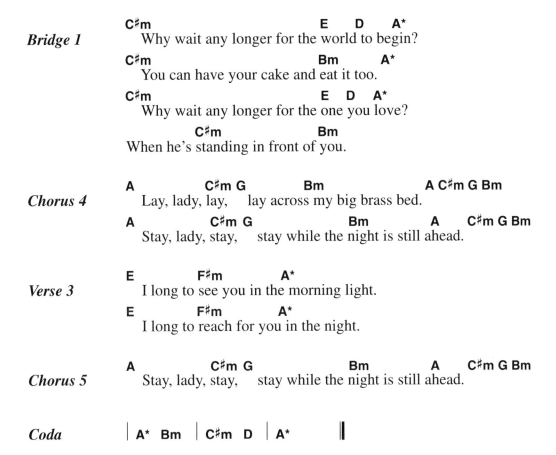

Bridge 1

C♯m   E   D   A*
Why wait any longer for the world to begin?

C♯m   Bm   A*
You can have your cake and eat it too.

C♯m   E   D   A*
Why wait any longer for the one you love?

           C♯m   Bm
When he's standing in front of you.

Chorus 4

A   C♯m G   Bm   A C♯m G Bm
Lay, lady, lay,   lay across my big brass bed.

A   C♯m G   Bm   A   C♯m G Bm
Stay, lady, stay,   stay while the night is still ahead.

Verse 3

E   F♯m   A*
I long to see you in the morning light.

E   F♯m   A*
I long to reach for you in the night.

Chorus 5

A   C♯m G   Bm   A   C♯m G Bm
Stay, lady, stay,   stay while the night is still ahead.

Coda

| A* Bm | C♯m D | A*   ‖

Tangled Up In Blue

from *Blood on the Tracks* (1975)

IN SEPTEMBER 1974, Bob Dylan flew into New York, telephoned his record company and said "let's do a record". A band was quickly found and Bob instructed them "I want to lay down a whole bunch of tracks. I don't want to overdub. I want it easy and natural." The resulting album, *Blood On The Tracks*, is still regarded by many as his finest. 'Tangled Up In Blue' is a great piece to play on guitar, due to its easy riff and full-sounding acoustic 12-string part.

Guitar parts
Take a listen to the CD and you'll hear two acoustic guitars. The six-string (played by Bob himself) is mainly heard in the left speaker. In the right speaker you'll hear the acoustic 12-string guitar part, which helps to add texture to the overall sound.

How to play it
The verse accompaniment (see TAB) consists of a single bass note of A, then a strum of the chord, then rapid up- and down-strums on a chord of A/G. Move your strumming hand in an even up and down motion, and try to keep your wrist relaxed – if you're tense you won't manage the rapid Asus4 chords that characterise the part. When the song changes to a chord of E ("I was standin' on the side of the road…") the strumming part is very similar, but you'll need to incorporate the slightly more difficult F♯m 2nd fret barre chord. Also, don't be tempted to slow down the strumming over the hook line "Tangled Up in Blue" – listen to the CD recording and you'll hear that it's just as fast over this section.

Capo tips
Although the original guitar part is played without a capo, you can try using one to simulate the effect of a 12-string. Put a capo at the 7th fret, and play the song with chord shapes based in the key of D. This is especially effective if you're playing the song unaccompanied with another guitarist covering the original part.

▼ Verse accompaniment

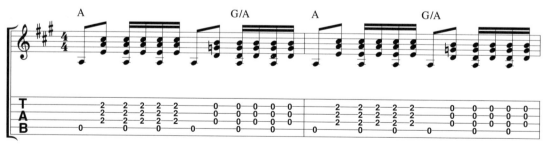

"You don't have to starve to be a good artist.
You just have to have love, insight
and a strong point of view."

9 Tangled Up In Blue

Words & Music by Bob Dylan

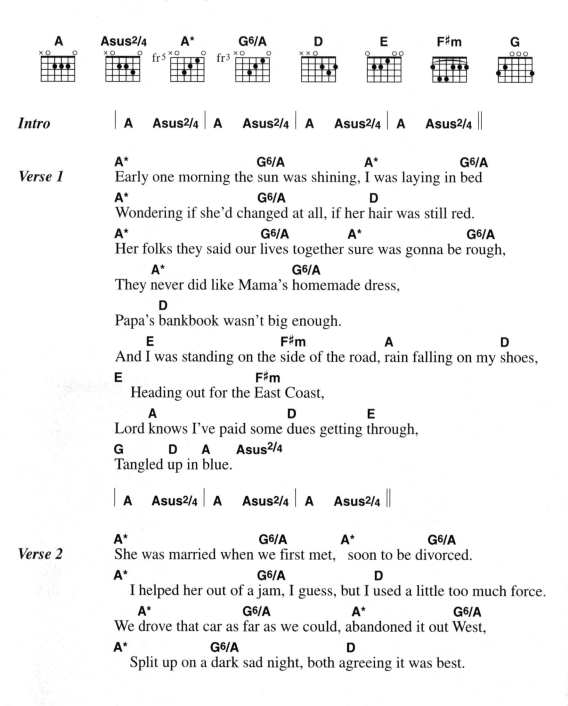

A **Asus2/4** fr5 **A*** fr3 **G6/A** **D** **E** **F♯m** **G**

Intro

| A Asus2/4 | A Asus2/4 | A Asus2/4 | A Asus2/4 ‖

Verse 1

  A*   **G6/A**   **A***   **G6/A**
Early one morning the sun was shining, I was laying in bed

  A*   **G6/A**   **D**
Wondering if she'd changed at all, if her hair was still red.

  A*   **G6/A**   **A***   **G6/A**
Her folks they said our lives together sure was gonna be rough,

        A*   **G6/A**
They never did like Mama's homemade dress,

      D
Papa's bankbook wasn't big enough.

         E   **F♯m**   **A**   **D**
And I was standing on the side of the road, rain falling on my shoes,

E   **F♯m**
     Heading out for the East Coast,

      A   **D**   **E**
Lord knows I've paid some dues getting through,

G   **D**   **A**   **Asus2/4**
Tangled up in blue.

| A Asus2/4 | A Asus2/4 | A Asus2/4 ‖

Verse 2

  A*   **G6/A**   **A***   **G6/A**
She was married when we first met,   soon to be divorced.

  A*   **G6/A**   **D**
   I helped her out of a jam, I guess, but I used a little too much force.

   A*   **G6/A**   **A***   **G6/A**
We drove that car as far as we could, abandoned it out West,

A*   **G6/A**   **D**
   Split up on a dark sad night, both agreeing it was best.

```
E                    F♯m        A            D
She turned around to look at me as I was walking away,
E                       F♯m
    I heard her say over my shoulder,
        A               D                E
"We'll meet again someday on the avenue,"
G      D    A    Asus²/⁴
Tangled up in blue.
```

| A   Asus2/4 | A   Asus2/4 | A   Asus2/4 ‖

Verse 3

```
A*               G6/A              A*                G6/A
I had a job in the great north woods working as a cook for a spell,
      A*          G6/A              D
But I never did like it all that much and one day the axe just fell.
      A*          G6/A                 A*          G6/A
So I drifted down to New Orleans where I happened to be employed
A*                      G6/A           D
Working for a while on a fishing boat right outside of Delacroix.
E                 F♯m        A            D
But all the while I was alone, the past was close behind,
E               F♯m        A           D              E
I seen a lot of women but she never escaped my mind, and I just grew
G      D    A    Asus²/⁴
Tangled up in blue.
```

| A   Asus2/4 | A   Asus2/4 | A   Asus2/4 ‖

Verse 4

```
A*                    G/6A            A*               G6/A
She was working in a topless place and I stopped in for a beer,
      A*              G6/A                 D
I just kept looking at the side of her face in the spotlight so clear.
      A*          G6/A
And later on when the crowd thinned out
    A*             G6/A
I's just about to do the same,
          A*            G6/A
She was standing there in back of my chair,
        D
Said to me, "Don't I know your name?"
E                       F♯m
I muttered something underneath my breath,
    A                    D
She studied the lines on my face.
```

47

cont.

```
      E                    F♯m
I must admit I felt a little uneasy
             A              D          E
When she bent down to tie the laces of my shoe,
G      D    A    Asus²/₄
Tangled up in blue.
```

```
| A    Asus²/₄ | A    Asus²/₄ | A    Asus²/₄ ‖
```

Verse 5

```
A*                G⁶/A            A*          G⁶/A
She lit a burner on the stove and offered me a pipe.
A*                     G⁶/A
"I thought you'd never say hello," she said,
        D
"You look like the silent type."
              A*          G⁶/A              A*        G⁶/A
Then she opened up a book of poems and handed it to me,
A*          G⁶/A              D
Written by an Italian poet from the thirteenth century.
        E              F♯m
And every one of them words rang true
      A              D
And glowed like burning coal,
E            F♯m
Pouring off of every page
          A          D            E
Like it was written in my soul from me to you,
G      D    A    Asus²/₄
Tangled up in blue.
```

```
| A    Asus²/₄ | A    Asus²/₄ | A    Asus²/₄ ‖
```

Verse 6

```
    A*              G⁶/A
I lived with them on Montague Street
      A*              G⁶/A
In a basement down the stairs,
          A*            G⁶/A
There was music in the cafés at night
          D
And revolution in the air.
```

    A*   **G6/A**
Then he started into dealing with slaves
    A*   **G6/A**
And something inside of him died.
  A*   **G6/A**   **D**
She had to sell everything she owned and froze up inside.
   E   **F♯m**   **A**   **D**
And when finally the bottom fell out I became withdrawn,
   E   **F♯m**
The only thing I knew how to do
    A   **D**   **E**
Was to keep on keeping on like a bird that flew,
G   **D** **A** **Asus2/4**
Tangled up in blue.

 | **A** **Asus2/4** | **A** **Asus2/4** | **A** **Asus2/4** ‖

   A*   **G6/A**   **A***   **G6/A**
So now I'm going back again, I got to get to her somehow.
A*   **G6/A**   **D**
All the people we used to know, they're an illusion to me now.
A*   **G6/A** **A***   **G6/A**
Some are mathematicians, some are carpenter's wives.
   A*   **G6/A**
Don't know how it all got started,
     D
I don't know what they're doing with their lives.
   E   **F♯m**   **A**   **D**
But me, I'm still on the road heading for another joint.
E   **F♯m**
We always did feel the same,
    A   **D** **E**
We just saw it from a different point of view,
G   **D** **A** **Asus4**
Tangled up in blue.

 | **A** **Asus4** | **A** **Asus4** | **A** **Asus4** ‖

 ‖: **A* G6/A** | **A* G6/A** | **A* G6/A** | **D**   :‖

 | **E** **F♯m** | **A** **D** | **E** **F♯m** | **A** **D** |

 | **E** | **G** **D** **A** ‖

You're A Big Girl Now

from *Blood On The Tracks* (1975)

THIS SAD TALE of love and loss finds Dylan in an unusually personal mood, echoing the sentiments of the classic blues songs that inspired a great deal of his work. As with much of the material on *Blood On The Tracks*, it was borne out of separation from his wife Sara (the song's subject is echoed in the track 'If You See Her, Say Hello').

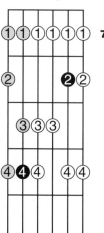

How to play it

The delicate acoustic guitar accompaniment is halfway between arpeggiated plectrum picking and gentle strumming, with subtle sections of guitar melody thrown in for good measure. Your accompaniment style should be based on four slow downstrokes per bar, throwing in occasional upstrokes in between these. Keep elbow movement to a minimum and pivot from the wrist throughout.

To vary the pattern, try adding arpeggiated (i.e. single-note) sections, plucking one string of the chord at a time. You can hear this on the CD in bar 5, when the G chord comes in. Additional melody parts (from both guitars) are improvised, using notes taken from the G major scale. We've shown this in its 7th fret position (see fretbox on this page), because it covers most of the range used, although both guitarists shift scale positions several times during the track.

More complex picking

As the song develops the picking becomes busier. We've notated two bars taken from verse 3 (see TAB) to show how the arrangement becomes more interesting in the later verses. Don't try to copy these picked notes exactly, but use them as a guide to developing a relaxed but intricate picking part that feels comfortable.

▼ Verse 3 excerpt

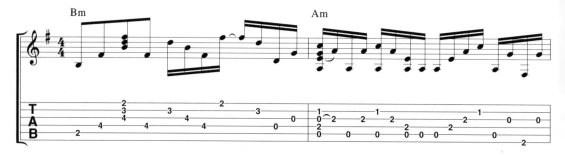

"I read that it was supposed to be about my wife –
well, I wish somebody would ask me first before
they print stuff like that. I mean, it couldn't be about
anyone else but my wife, right?"

10 You're A Big Girl Now

Words & Music by Bob Dylan

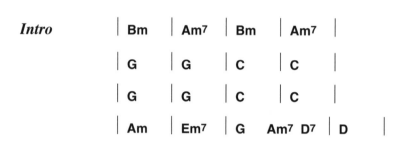

Bm   Em7   Am7   G   C   Em7

Intro

Bm	Am7	Bm	Am7
G	G	C	C
G	G	C	C
Am	Em7	G Am7 D7	D

Verse 1

Bm   Am7
 Our conversation was short and sweet

Bm   Am7
 It nearly swept me off-a my feet.

      G   C
And I'm back in the rain, oh, oh,

        G
And you are on dry land.

C   Am
 You made it there somehow

Bm   Am7   G D
 You're a big girl now.

Verse 2

Bm   Am7
 Bird on the horizon, sittin' on a fence,

Bm   Am7
 He's singin' his song for me at his own expense.

      G   C
And I'm just like that bird, oh, oh,

       G
Singin' just for you.

C   Am7
 I hope that you can hear,

Bm   Am7   G D
 Hear me singin' through these tears.

Verse 3

Bm   Am⁷

  Time is a jet plane, it moves too fast

Bm   Am⁷

  Oh, but what a shame that all we've shared can't last.

      G   C

I can change, I swear, oh, oh,

           G

See what you can do.

C   Am

  I can make it through,

Bm Am   G D

  You can make it too.

Verse 4

Bm   Am⁷

  Love is so simple, to quote a phrase,

Bm   Am⁷

  You've known it all the time, I'm learnin' it these days.

      G   C

Oh, I know where I can find you, oh, oh,

          G

In somebody's room.

C   Am⁷

  It's a price I have to pay

Bm   G D

  You're a big girl all the way.

Verse 5

Bm   Am⁷

  A change in the weather is known to be extreme

Bm   Am⁷

  But what's the sense of changing horses in midstream?

      G   C

I'm going out of my mind, oh, oh,

          G

With a pain that stops and starts

C   Am⁷

  Like a corkscrew to my heart

Bm   Am⁷   G D

  Ever since we've been apart.

Solo

| Bm | Am⁷ | Bm | Am⁷ | |

| G | C | G | C | |

| Am | Em⁷ | G Am⁷ D⁷ | D | | *To fade*

53

Cold Irons Bound

from *Time Out of Mind* (1997)

'COLD IRONS BOUND' is taken from Dylan's 1997 album *Time Out Of Mind*, and it was the second time he had used legendary producer Daniel Lanois. Dylan was actively looking for a classic blues sound – he even played Lanois early blues recordings to give him an idea how the album should sound.

▼ A blues scale with capo

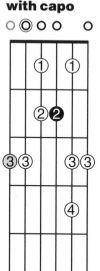

How to play it

The song sounds in the key of B♭, but all the chord shapes and riffs make use of open strings, so you'll need to put a capo on the first fret and play chords in the key of A to get the right sound. The distorted guitar chord accompaniment comes in at 0:20 on the CD recording, playing a repeating pattern of D U U U (see TAB) – listen to the CD at this point to get the exact timing. Note that Bob uses a slightly unusual version of the A7 chord, with the third fret on the first (thinnest) string added to a regular chord of A.

Improvising

Apart from the bass riff, there is very little repeated material in the track, because all the guitar parts are improvised from the blues scale. In the fretbox opposite we've shown the notes in the open A blues scale (which is actually B♭ blues on the recording – so use a 1st fret capo for this too). Throughout the song, Bob improvises bluesy lines (see the example in the TAB), focussing mainly on the lower-pitched notes of the scale. Session guitarist Duke Robillard plays the higher-sounding notes using a fretted position of the same scale.

Guitar sound

As with most classic electric blues guitar, the sound should be slightly distorted, but not so far that it becomes a rock tone. Interestingly, the rhythm guitar is more distorted than the lead part. The twangy low notes should be almost clean, with the bridge pickup selected and lots of reverb added. Try picking with the plectrum close to the bridge for an even more pronounced attack to the notes.

▼ Intro excerpt

Cold Irons Bound

Words & Music by Bob Dylan

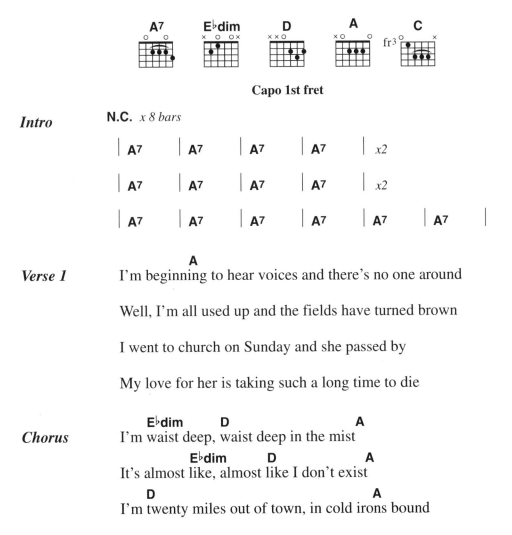

Capo 1st fret

Intro

N.C. *x 8 bars*

| A⁷ | A⁷ | A⁷ | A⁷ | *x2* |

| A⁷ | A⁷ | A⁷ | A⁷ | *x2* |

| A⁷ | A⁷ | A⁷ | A⁷ | A⁷ | A⁷ | |

Verse 1

              A
I'm beginning to hear voices and there's no one around

Well, I'm all used up and the fields have turned brown

I went to church on Sunday and she passed by

My love for her is taking such a long time to die

Chorus

        E♭dim   D   A
I'm waist deep, waist deep in the mist
            E♭dim   D   A
It's almost like, almost like I don't exist
        D   A
I'm twenty miles out of town, in cold irons bound

Cold Irons Bound

Verse 2

The walls of pride are high and wide

Can't see over to the other side

It's such a sad thing to see beauty decay

It's sadder still, to feel your heart torn away

Chorus 2

         E♭dim G   A
One look at you   and I'm out of control
      E♭dim   D   A
Like the universe has swallowed me whole
        D   C   A
I'm twenty miles out of town in Cold irons bound

Verse 3

There's too many people, too many to recall

I thought some of 'm were friends of mine; I was wrong about 'm all

Well, the road is rocky and the hillside's mud

Up over my head nothing but clouds of blood

Chorus 3

        E♭dim D   A
I found my world, found my world in you
        E♭dim D   A
But your love   just hasn't proved true
        D   C   A
I'm twenty miles out of town in cold irons bound
D   C   A
Twenty miles out of town in cold irons bound

Solo

Chords as Verse

Verse 4	Oh, the winds in Chicago have torn me to shreds
	Reality has always had too many heads
	Some things last longer than you think they will
	There are some kind of things you can never kill

Chorus 4

      E♭dim   D   A
It's you and you only, I'm been thinking about
        E♭dim   D   A
But you can't see in and it's hard lookin' out
            D   C   A
I'm twenty miles out of town in cold irons bound

Verse 5	Well the fat's in the fire and the water's in the tank
	The whiskey's in the jar and the money's in the bank
	I tried to love and protect you because I cared
	I'm gonna remember forever the joy that we shared

Chorus 5

        E♭dim   D   A
Looking at you and I'm on my bended knee
      E♭dim D   A
You have no idea what you do to me

I'm twenty miles out of town in cold irons bound
D   C   A
Twenty miles out of town in cold irons bound

Outro   *Solo on* **A⁷** *to fade*

12 Things Have Changed

from *The Essential Bob Dylan* (2000)

DYLAN HAS BEEN associated with film throughout his career, as an actor, producer or composer, or just appearing as himself. In 2000 he won the Best Song Oscar for 'Things Have Changed', written for the film *Wonder Boys*. It appeared on the 2000 album *The Essential Bob Dylan*.

▼ Em pentatonic scale with capo

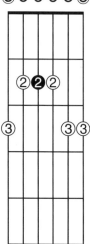

How to play it

Use a capo at the 3rd fret so that when you play the easy chords of Em, Am, B7 etc they will sound right with the original recording (actually in the key of Gm). The strumming pattern consists of simple down- and up-strokes throughout, though Bob occasionally makes use of percussive palm mutes. This technique involves stopping the strings from sounding by slapping the palm onto the strings near the bridge when strumming. It's very subtle on the original recording, so if you find that it restricts your movement, just strum more lightly than you usually would. Try to avoid striking all of the strings, all of the time, so you've got the flexibility to add variations in the texture of the chord part.

Lead guitar

If you listen very carefully to the CD you'll hear that there is an acoustic lead guitar part that plays throughout the song. It's an improvisation that uses notes taken from the Em pentatonic scale (see fretbox) – note that this guitar also uses a 3rd fret capo. When you try out your own soloing ideas over the backing track, keep the riffs simple, and don't play up and down the whole scale for every phrase – note that the original's phrases are often just two or three notes.

▼ Rhythm guitar part

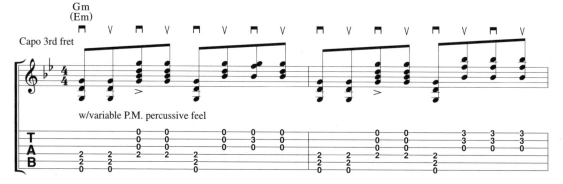

"I'm not doing it to see how good I can sound,
or how perfect the melody can be,
or how intricate the details can be woven
or how perfectly written something can be.
I don't care about those things."

13 Things Have Changed

Words & Music by Bob Dylan

| Em | Am | B7 | C |

Capo third fret

Intro | Em | Em | Em | Em ||

Verse 1
Em
A worried man with a worried mind,
Am
No one in front of me and nothing behind.
Em   B7
There's a woman on my lap and she's drinking champagne,
Em
Got white skin, got assassin's eyes.
Am
I'm looking up into the sapphire tinted skies,
Em   B7 Em
I'm well dressed, waiting on the last   train.

Pre-chorus 1
C   B7   Em
Standing on the gallows with my head in a noose,
C   B7
Any minute now I'm expecting all hell to break   loose.

Chorus 1
Em
People are crazy and times are strange,
Am
I'm locked in tight, I'm out of range,
Em   B7   Em
I used to care but things have changed.

Link 1 | Em | Em | Am | Am |

| Em | Em B7 | Em | Em ||

Verse 2

Em
This place ain't doing me any good,

Am
I'm in the wrong town, I should be in Hollywood.

Em   B7
Just for a second there I thought I saw something move.

Em
Gonna take dancing lessons, do the jitterbug rag,

Am
Ain't no shortcuts, gonna dress in drag,

Em   B7   Em
Only a fool in here would think he's got anything to prove.

Pre-chorus 2

C   B7   Em
Lot of water under the bridge, lot of other stuff too,

C   B7
Don't get up gentlemen, I'm only passing through.

Chorus 2

Em
People are crazy and times are strange,

Am
I'm locked in tight, I'm out of range,

Em   B7   Em
I used to care but things have changed.

Link 2

| Em | Em | Am | Am |

| Em | Em B7 | Em | Em   ‖

Verse 3

Em
I've been walking forty miles of bad road,

Am
If the Bible is right, the world will explode.

Em   B7
I've been trying to get as far away from myself as I can.

Em
   Some things are too hot to touch,

Am
   The human mind can only stand so much,

Em   B7   Em
You can't win with a losing   hand.

Pre-chorus 3

C   B7   Em
Feel like falling in love with the first woman I meet,

C   B7
Putting her in a wheel barrow and wheeling her down the street.

Things Have Changed

Chorus 3

Em
People are crazy and times are strange,

   Am
I'm locked in tight, I'm out of range,

Em   **B7**   **Em**
I used to care but things have changed.

Link 4

| Em | Em | Am | Am | |

| Em | Em **B7** | Em | Em | ‖

Verse 4

Em
I hurt easy, I just don't show it,

   Am
You can hurt someone and not even know it.

Em   **B7**
The next sixty seconds could be like an eternity,

   Em
Gonna get low down, gonna fly high,

   Am
All the truth in the world adds up to one big lie.

Em   **B7** **Em**
I'm in love with a woman who don't even appeal to me.

Pre-chorus 4

  C   **B7**   **Em**
Mr. Jinx and Miss Lucy, they jumped in the lake,

C   **B7**
  I'm not that eager to make a mistake.

Chorus 4

Em
People are crazy and times are strange,

   Am
I'm locked in tight, I'm out of range,

Em   **B7**   **Em**
I used to care but things have changed.

Coda

| Em | Em | Am | Am | |

| Em | Em **B7** ‖

Fade out

"I tend to base all my songs on the old songs, like the old folk songs, the old blues tunes; they are always good. They always make sense."

Further Reading

If you've enjoyed this book why not check out some of the great titles below. They are available from all good music retailers and book shops, or you can visit our website: www.musicsales.com. In case of difficulty please contact Music Sales direct (see page 2).

The Chord Songbook Series

Play all your favourite hits with just a few easy chords for each song! Huge range of titles to choose from, including:

NEW! **Abba** AM959740
The Beatles NO90664
Blur AM936914
Bon Jovi AM936892
Boyzone AM956956
Bryan Adams AM963490
Eric Clapton AM956054
The Corrs AM956967
The Cranberries AM944383
Bob Dylan AM959706
The Levellers AM951445
Metallica AM944680
Alanis Morissette AM944086
Oasis AM936903
Oasis 2 AM951478

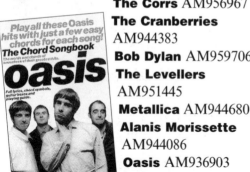

Pulp AM942678
Paul Simon PS11485
Stereophonics AM956065
Sting AM940489
Stone Roses AM951500
Paul Weller AM942546
Wet Wet Wet AM938135
The Who AM956021

Play Guitar With...Series

Play guitar and sing along with the specially-recorded CD backing tracks for classic songs from your favourite bands. Here are just some of the titles in this superb series.

The Beatles NO90665
The Beatles Book 2 NO90667
The Beatles Book 3 NO90689
Blur AM935320
Bon Jovi AM92558
Bryan Adams AM963380
Eric Clapton AM950862
Eric Clapton Book 2 AM96289
Bob Dylan AM955944
The Kinks AM951863
Kula Shaker AM943767
Metallica AM92559
Oasis AM935330
Ocean Colour Scene AM943712
Simon & Garfunkel PS11516
Paul Simon PS11469
Sting AM968000
The Stone Roses AM943701

...plus many more titles for you to collect!

02/07 (61274)